Big League Peanuts

P9-CAL-436

Big League Peanuts

by Charles M. Schulz

An Owl Book

Holt, Rinehart and Winston/New York

Copyright © 1985 by United Feature Syndicate, Inc.
Based on the PEANUTS ® comic strip by Charles M. Schulz.
All rights reserved, including the right to reproduce this book or portions thereof in any form.
Published by Holt, Rinehart and Winston, 383 Madison Avenue, New York, New York 10017.
Published simultaneously in Canada by Holt, Rinehart and Winston of Canada, Limited.

Library of Congress Catalog Card Number: 85-60951
ISBN: 0-03-004428-6

First Edition

Printed in the United States of America
10 9 8 7 6 5 4 3 2 1

ISBN 0-03-004428-6

TODAY'S SPRING-TRAINING SESSION IS GOING TO BEGIN WITH A DEMONSTRATION..

LAST YEAR WE HIT INTO TOO MANY DOUBLE-PLAYS...

TWO OF OUR MEMBERS ARE GOING TO SHOW US HOW THIS CAN BE AVOIDED...

LINUS IS GOING TO BE THE SHORTSTOP, AND SNOOPY IS GOING TO BE THE RUNNER GOING FROM FIRST TO SECOND WHO BREAKS UP THE DOUBLE-PLAY...

NOW, WATCH CAREFULLY.. THE PLAY BEGINS WITH LINUS FIELDING THE BALL AND MAKING THE PLAY AT SECOND WHILE SNOOPY STREAKS TOWARD HIM..

AAUGH!!!

ARE THERE ANY QUESTIONS?

SCHULZ

ALL RIGHT, TEAM...LET'S PAY ATTENTION NOW!

WE HAVE A LONG HARD SEASON AHEAD OF US! I'M NOT OFFERING YOU AN EASY TASK! I'M GOING TO ASK FOR **SACRIFICE, HARD WORK AND DEDICATION!**

I'M GOING TO ASK THAT YOU DRIVE YOURSELVES TO THE VERY LIMITS OF ENDURANCE!

PLEASE?

IT'S NOT FAIR FOR YOU TO ASK US TO SACRIFICE, WORK HARD AND BE DEDICATED!

WE JUST WANT TO WIN BALL GAMES...WE DON'T WANT TO SUFFER!

ALL YOU LEADERS ARE ALIKE!! YOU'RE ALWAYS TRYING TO STIR US UP! WHY DON'T YOU JUST LEAD US, AND STOP BOTHERING US?

YES, WHAT ARE YOU TRYING TO DO, MAKE US **NERVOUS**?!

Z

BONK

WELL! DID THAT NASTY OL' POP FLY AWAKEN YOU? DID IT DISTURB YOUR BEAUTY SLEEP?

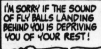

I'M SORRY IF THE SOUND OF FLY BALLS LANDING BEHIND YOU IS DEPRIVING YOU OF YOUR REST!

PERHAPS WE SHOULD SOFTEN THE INFIELD SO THE BALL WON'T MAKE SO MUCH NOISE WHEN IT LANDS BEHIND YOU...

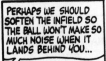

WAAH!

OH, GOOD GRIEF! NOW, I'VE HURT HIS FEELINGS...

I'M SORRY, SNOOPY.. I APOLOGIZE.. I SHOULDN'T HAVE BEEN SO SARCASTIC.. I GUESS I DON'T KNOW HOW TO HANDLE PLAYERS...I'M A TERRIBLE MANAGER... I APOLOGIZE..

SNIF

Z

BONK

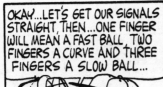

WHAT'S THIS? YOU'RE GOING TO THROW HIM A CURVE?

THIS IS NO TIME TO BE THROWING A CURVE... A KNUCKLE BALL IS THE PITCH... A KNUCKLE BALL WILL CATCH HIM FLAT-FOOTED!

?!

WHY DON'T I JUST FIX YOUR FINGERS HERE SO YOU CAN CATCH THIS GUY FLAT-FOOTED WITH A KNUCKLE BALL?

THERE! AND NOW WE'LL GIVE EACH LITTLE FINGER A KISS FOR GOOD LUCK... ♡♡ KISS! KISS! KISS! KISS!

AND ONE EXTRA LITTLE OL' KISS FOR THE THUMB! ♡

SMAK!

IF YOU DON'T GET BACK IN CENTERFIELD WHERE YOU BELONG, I'M GONNA BREAK ALL YOUR ARMS!

HE'LL APOLOGIZE WHEN THE KNUCKLE BALL CATCHES THAT GUY FLAT-FOOTED...

GOOD AFTERNOON...
MY NAME IS LUCY..

I'M GOING TO BE YOUR
RIGHT FIELDER... OUR
SPECIAL TODAY IS A
MISJUDGED FLY BALL

WE ALSO HAVE A NICE
BOBBLED GROUND BALL
AND AN EXCELLENT LATE
THROW TO THE INFIELD...

I'LL BE BACK IN
A MOMENT TO
TAKE YOUR ORDER

I WONDER
WHAT HE'S GOING
TO PITCH TO THIS
NEXT HITTER...

PROBABLY A
CURVE BALL

PSST, CHARLIE BROWN.....WE
OUTFIELDERS HAVE BEEN WONDERING
WHAT YOU'RE GOING TO PITCH TO THIS GUY...

A
CURVE
BALL

REALLY?

YOU WERE RIGHT! HE'S GONNA
THROW HIM THE CURVE BALL!

WHAT WAS THAT LAST PITCH YOU THREW, CHARLIE BROWN? THAT GUY MISSED IT A MILE!

THAT WAS THE OL' SCHMUCKLE BALL..LUCY INVENTED IT...

YOU JUST SORT OF SCHMUSH YOUR KNUCKLES AROUND THE BALL LIKE THIS AND THEN THROW IT AS HARD AS YOU CAN

EVERY TIME IT WORKS I GET A ROYALTY!

THIS NEXT GUY IS STRONG, CHARLIE BROWN

DON'T THROW HIM ANYTHING HE CAN HIT...

I HATE TO DISTURB YOU, BUT IF YOU'RE GOING TO SLEEP ON SECOND BASE, IT'S GOING TO PUT A LOT OF EXTRA PRESSURE ON ME AS PITCHER...

YOU SEE, I'LL HAVE TO TRY TO HOLD THEIR HITTERS TO SINGLES, AND I'M NOT SURE I CAN DO THAT...IF ONE OF THEIR HITTERS GETS TO ME FOR A DOUBLE OR A TRIPLE OR A HOME RUN, YOU KNOW WHAT'S GOING TO HAPPEN?

HE'S GONNA STOMP RIGHT ON YOUR STOMACH!!

THAT'S WHAT IS KNOWN AS MEANINGFUL DIALOGUE

LOOK, LUCY, THIS IS OUR LAST GAME OF THE SEASON..

CAN'T YOU PLAY ANY BETTER THAN YOU'VE BEEN PLAYING?

YOU'VE DROPPED FIVE FLY BALLS THIS INNING!

YOUR CAP IS TOUCHING MY CAP, CHARLIE BROWN...

MOVE YOUR HEAD SO YOUR CAP WON'T TOUCH MY CAP...

WHENEVER A MANAGER TALKS TO ONE OF HIS PLAYERS, HE SHOULD MAKE SURE THAT HIS CAP DOESN'T TOUCH THE PLAYER'S CAP...

I CAN'T STAND IT!

SCHULZ

I'VE BEEN GOING OVER OUR TEAM RECORDS, CHARLIE BROWN...

WE LOST EVERY GAME THIS SEASON!

MAYBE WE'RE BUILDING CHARACTER

SCHULZ

HERE'S SOMETHING I THINK ABOUT QUITE OFTEN..

I'M SITTING IN THE STANDS AT THE BALL GAME, SEE...SUDDENLY A LINE DRIVE IS HIT MY WAY..EVERYBODY DUCKS, BUT I STICK UP MY HAND, AND MAKE A GREAT CATCH!

THE MANAGER OF THE HOME TEAM SEES ME AND YELLS, "SIGN THAT KID UP!"

HAVE YOU EVER HEARD OF ANYONE ELSE HAVING THAT DREAM?

ONLY ABOUT THIRTY BILLION OTHER KIDS!

NO WONDER YOU WANT TO BE THE PITCHER, CHARLIE BROWN...IT'S COOL UP HERE ON THE PITCHER'S MOUND!

YOU SHOULD FEEL HOW HOT IT IS OUT THERE IN CENTER FIELD...WE DON'T GET ANY BREEZE AT ALL..

HEY, GIRLS, COME UP HERE! FEEL THE COOL BREEZE!

STRIKE THREE!

I SHOULD GET **FOUR** STRIKES BECAUSE I'M A GIRL!

STRIKE FOUR

YOU SHOULD GIVE ME **FIVE** STRIKES BECAUSE I WAS SICK YESTERDAY...

STRIKE FIVE!

I SHOULD GET **SIX** STRIKES BECAUSE I'M SO CUTE...

WHAT KIND OF A STUPID GAME IS IT WHERE YOU ONLY GET FIVE STRIKES?

I HAVE A NEW AMBITION...

WHEN I GET BIG, I'D LIKE TO BE A BASEBALL UMPIRE...

WHAT IN THE WORLD MAKES YOU THINK YOU COULD BE A GOOD BASEBALL UMPIRE?

BECAUSE I'M ALWAYS RIGHT!

EVERYBODY CAN GO HOME! IT LOOKS LIKE IT ISN'T GOING TO STOP RAINING...EVERYBODY CAN GO HOME!

IT'S HARD TO TELL EVERYBODY TO GO HOME WHEN NO ONE SHOWED UP!

AHEM!

!

RIGHT IN THE MIDDLE OF A BALL GAME?

ARE YOU OUT OF YOUR MIND?!

I'M TRYING TO PITCH, CAN'T YOU SEE THAT ?!!! I'VE GOT TO CONCENTRATE ON WHAT I'M DOING!

OH, NOW YOU'RE GOING TO BE HURT, AREN'T YOU ? OH, GOOD GRIEF, ALL RIGHT... COME HERE...

SKRITCH
SKRITCH
SKRITCH
SKRITCH
SKRITCH

✳ SIGH! ✳

NO WONDER SANDY KOUFAX RETIRED!

COME ON, CHARLIE BROWN, STRIKE HIM OUT!

I KNOW YOU LIKE LOTS OF CHATTER OUT THERE, MANAGER, BUT I CAN'T THINK OF ANYTHING TO CHATTER...

WELL, HOW ABOUT SAYING, "THROW IT BY 'IM, PITCHER," OR HOW ABOUT, "HE CAN'T HIT WHAT HE CAN'T SEE!"

ANOTHER GOOD ONE IS, "SHOW 'IM THE HIGH, HARD ONE!"

COULD YOU WRITE SOME OF THOSE DOWN? I'LL NEVER BE ABLE TO REMEMBER THEM OTHERWISE

THANK YOU... THIS WILL BE A BIG HELP..

"OKAY, PITCHER, THROW IT PAST HIM! HE CAN'T HIT WHAT HE CAN'T SEE!"

"PITCH HARD, CHARLIE BROWN!"

"STAY WITH 'IM, KID! YOU CAN DO IT, CHARLIE BROWN! BE GOOD BOY! GOOD SHOT! SHOW 'IM THE HIGH, HARD ONE.."

SIGH

BONK

AAUGH!

I CAN'T STAND IT

WHAT KIND OF AN OUTFIELDER ARE YOU?!

THAT BALL ONLY MISSED YOU BY A FOOT!! CAN'T YOU **SEE**? WHAT WERE YOU THINKING ABOUT? WHAT'S WRONG WITH YOU?!

YOU'RE GETTING WORSE ALL THE TIME! WHAT DO YOU WANT THEM TO DO, COME OUT HERE AND HAND YOU THE BALL?

WHAT IN THE WORLD MADE YOU MISS THAT ONE?!!

I WAS HAVING MY QUIET TIME!

SCHULZ

WHAT'S THE SCORE NOW, MANAGER?

WE'RE BEHIND FIFTY-SEVEN TO NOTHING!

WHY DON'T WE JUST SORT OF SLIP AWAY, AND GO HOME, AND WATCH TV OR SOMETHING?

MANAGERS NEVER LIKE TO TAKE SUGGESTIONS!

I GOT IT!

I GOT IT! I GOT IT!

"I GOT IT" CAN MEAN A LOT OF THINGS!

PERHAPS YOU SHOULDN'T BE A PLAYING MANAGER, CHARLIE BROWN..PERHAPS YOU SHOULD BE A BENCH MANAGER..

THAT'S A GOOD IDEA... YOU'D BE A GREAT BENCH MANAGER, CHARLIE BROWN...

YOU COULD SAY, "BENCH, DO THIS! BENCH, DO THAT!" YOU COULD EVEN BE IN CHARGE OF WHERE WE PUT THE BENCH..

WHEN THE TEAM GETS TO THE BALL PARK, YOU COULD SAY, "LET'S PUT THE BENCH HERE!" OR, "LET'S PUT THE BENCH THERE!"

I CAN'T STAND IT!

PRACTICE?! WHY DO WE HAVE TO PRACTICE? WE NEVER WIN ANY GAMES...

WHAT ARE WE GONNA DO, PRACTICE OUR LOSING?!

THAT WAS JUST A LITTLE JOKE!

I THINK YOU NEED A LITTLE PRACTICE ON FLY BALLS, LUCY, SO IF YOU'LL GET OUT THERE, I'LL HIT YOU A FEW...

JUST TROT ON OUT THERE, AND I'LL HIT SOME HIGH ONES, AND WE'LL SEE HOW YOU DO...

WELL, GO ON! GET OUT THERE BEFORE I HIT ONE AND YOU HAVE TO CHASE IT!

I'M WARNING YOU.. I'M NOT GONNA WAIT! I'LL JUST GO AHEAD AND WHACK ONE SO FAR YOU'LL HAVE TO RUN FIFTY MILES!

GO AHEAD! GET MOVING! GET OUT THERE BEFORE I SWING BECAUSE I'M NOT WAITING ANOTHER SECOND!

YOU'D BETTER START MOVING.. HERE IT GOES!!

SCHULZ

POW!

CHASE IT YOURSELF! YOU WERE THE ONE WHO PITCHED IT!!

✳ SIGH ✳

HEY, KID! YOU WITH THE BASEBALL GLOVE! Y'WANNA PLAY RIGHT FIELD? WE'RE SHORT A PLAYER!

WELL, I'M ALREADY IN A..

Y'WANNA PLAY OR NOT? GET OUT THERE! WE'RE READY TO START!

I'LL BE INTERESTED IN SEEING HOW THIS LOOKS IN THE BOX SCORE...

BAD NEWS, CHUCK...

MY TEAM CAN'T PLAY YOUR TEAM TODAY.. WE HAVE TOO MANY GUYS WHO AREN'T FEELING WELL....WE'RE GOING TO HAVE TO FORFEIT THE GAME

YOU WIN, CHUCK

ALL RIGHT, TEAM ...I DON'T WANT ANY LETDOWN NOW.. WE'VE GOT A STREAK GOING!

HELLO, CHARLIE BROWN? THIS IS FRANKLIN..

WE WON'T BE ABLE TO PLAY YOUR TEAM TODAY...FIVE OF OUR GUYS CAN'T MAKE IT...

WE'LL JUST HAVE TO FORFEIT THE GAME.... YOU WIN, CHARLIE BROWN..

I CAN'T BELIEVE IT.... A TWO-GAME WINNING STREAK

WOW!

I'VE BEEN STUDYING THE STANDINGS, CHARLIE BROWN..

THIS IS THE BEST SEASON WE'VE EVER HAD..

ONE MORE FORFEIT AND WE'LL BE IN FIRST PLACE!

JUST THINK.. WE'VE WON TWO GAMES IN A ROW BY FORFEIT..

IF THIS OTHER TEAM DOESN'T SHOW UP TODAY, WE'LL HAVE A THREE-GAME WINNING STREAK, AND WE'LL BE IN FIRST PLACE! WE'LL BE ON TOP OF THE LEAGUE! WE'LL BE THE..

HERE COMES THE OTHER TEAM

THUS ENDETH THE WINNING STREAK!

STRIKE THREE!

RATS!

I'LL NEVER BE A BIG-LEAGUE PLAYER! I JUST DON'T HAVE IT! ALL MY LIFE I'VE DREAMED OF PLAYING IN THE BIG LEAGUES, BUT I KNOW I'LL NEVER MAKE IT...

YOU'RE THINKING TOO FAR AHEAD, CHARLIE BROWN...WHAT YOU NEED TO DO IS TO SET YOURSELF MORE IMMEDIATE GOALS...

IMMEDIATE GOALS? YES

START WITH THIS NEXT INNING WHEN YOU GO OUT TO PITCH..

SEE IF YOU CAN WALK OUT TO THE MOUND WITHOUT FALLING DOWN!

SCHULZ

YOU KNOW WHAT OUR TEAM LACKED LAST YEAR?

IT LACKED ORGANIZATION! WELL, THIS YEAR IT'S GOING TO BE DIFFERENT!

I'VE WRITTEN DOWN THE NAME OF EACH PLAYER AND WHAT POSITION HE PLAYS, AND I'VE ATTACHED THE PAPERS TO A CLIP-BOARD...

IF THAT ISN'T ORGANIZATION, I DON'T KNOW WHAT IS!

LUCY, HOW WOULD YOU LIKE TO PLAY SECOND BASE?

NOT ON YOUR LIFE!! I'VE GOT TOO MUCH PRIDE!

WELL, WHAT IN THE WORLD IS WRONG WITH SECOND BASE?

SECOND BASE? OH, PARDON ME... I THOUGHT YOU SAID "SECOND FIDDLE"!

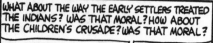

CHARLIE BROWN, I CAN'T PLAY CENTER FIELD ANY MORE..

WHY NOT?
THE WEEDS ARE TOO TALL OUT THERE!

OH, GOOD GRIEF STOP COMPLAINING, AND GET GOING!
ALL RIGHT..

BUT SOMEBODY BETTER TELL ME WHEN THE INNING IS OVER!

TIME OUT....THERE'S A BUG CROSSING THE INFIELD...

WHY DO YOU ALWAYS PUT YOUR LEFT SHOE ON FIRST, BIG BROTHER?

WELL, ACTUALLY, I DON'T... I ONLY PUT IT ON FIRST ON DAYS WHEN WE HAVE A BASEBALL GAME...

I GUESS IT'S KIND OF A SUPERSTITION... BASEBALL PLAYERS HAVE A LOT OF SUPERSTITIONS..

WHAT WOULD HAPPEN IF YOU DIDN'T DO IT?

WELL, WE'D PROBABLY LOSE THE GAME

HAVE YOU EVER WON?

WHERE'S OUR PITCHER?

I DON'T KNOW... I HAVEN'T SEEN HIM..

!?

I DON'T UNDERSTAND... THE GAME IS READY TO START, AND YOU'RE STILL SITTING HERE IN YOUR BEDROOM WITHOUT YOUR SHOES ON!

SCHULZ

EDUCATIONAL COSTS ARE REALLY GOING UP...

MY DAD SAYS IT CAN COST ALMOST SIXTEEN THOUSAND DOLLARS TO GO TO COLLEGE

I'M HOPING FOR A BASEBALL SCHOLARSHIP...

HA HA HA HA!

I DIDN'T EVEN KNOW SHE WAS LISTENING...

YOU DON'T THINK I CARE ABOUT ALL THE GAMES WE LOSE, DO YOU, CHARLIE BROWN?

WELL, I'LL HAVE YOU KNOW THAT I SPEND A LOT OF TIME OUT HERE IN CENTER FIELD, AND MOST OF IT IS SPENT CRYING...

SEE? THE GRASS IS EXTRA GREEN ALL AROUND THIS SPOT WHERE I STAND AND WATER IT WITH MY TEARS...

THAT'S VERY TOUCHING..

WE'RE MISSING SECOND BASE TODAY SO I THOUGHT WE COULD USE SNOOPY'S DISH..

I GUESS THAT'LL DO ALL RIGHT FOR PRACTICE

WAP!

POW

THIS IS GOING TO BE ONE OF THOSE DAYS WHEN WE GET NOTHING BUT SINGLES

HEY, PITCHER!

TELL YOUR CATCHER THAT THE GIRLS IN THE OUTFIELD HAVE JUST VOTED HIM AS THE CUTEST THING THIS SIDE OF HEAVEN!

HEY, CATCHER! THE GIRLS IN THE OUTFIELD HAVE JUST VOTED YOU AS THE CUTEST THING THIS SIDE OF HEAVEN!

HE SAID, "THANK YOU"

HE ALSO SAYS MAYBE YOU SHOULD PLAY A LITTLE DEEPER... MOVE BACK A LITTLE...

LIKE MAYBE FIFTY MILES!!

SCHULZ

HEY, PITCHER, I'M A REPORTER FOR THE SCHOOL PAPER...

WHAT DO YOU THINK ABOUT WHEN YOU'RE STANDING OUT HERE ON THE MUD PILE?

THE MUD PILE?

I'LL PUT DOWN THAT HE WAS A LONELY LOOKING FIGURE AS HE STOOD THERE ON THE MUD PILE...

THE MUD PILE?

HEY, CATCHER, HOW ABOUT AN INTERVIEW FOR OUR SCHOOL PAPER?

WHAT ABOUT ALL THIS EQUIPMENT YOU WEAR?

DOES IT REALLY PROTECT YOU?

WHAP

OFFHAND, I'D SAY IT DOESN'T

"THIS REPORTER HAS NEVER INTERVIEWED A WORSE BASEBALL TEAM"

"THE MANAGER IS INEPT AND THE PLAYERS ARE HOPELESS"

"WE WILL SAY, HOWEVER, THAT THE CATCHER IS KIND OF CUTE, AND THE RIGHT FIELDER, WHO HAS DARK HAIR, IS VERY BEAUTIFUL"

GOOD ARTICLE, HUH?

HERE WE GO... THE FIRST PITCH OF THE NEW SEASON...

POW!

SOMETIMES I HAVE DIFFICULTY TELLING ONE SEASON FROM ANOTHER...

SNOOPY HAS BEEN CHOSEN "ROOKIE OF THE YEAR"!

LOOK AT THE TROPHY THEY GAVE HIM! AND THE BRONZE PLAQUE! CONGRATULATIONS, SNOOPY! YOU DESERVED IT!

WOW! ONE OF MY OWN PLAYERS..ROOKIE OF THE YEAR! ISN'T THAT SOMETHING?

OKAY, TEAM! THAT PROVES WE'RE NOT SO BAD AFTER ALL! LET'S GET OUT THERE NOW AND WIN THIS GAME...LET'S SHOW 'EM HOW TO PLAY!

BONK!

I KNOW WHAT AWARD I'LL WIN.."STOMACH-ACHE OF THE YEAR"!

I'VE MADE A BIG DECISION...

THIS IS THE TIME OF YEAR WHEN ALL THE BIG BASEBALL TRADES ARE MADE...I'M GOING TO TRY TO IMPROVE OUR TEAM WITH A FEW SHREWD TRADES

THAT'S A GREAT IDEA, CHARLIE BROWN...

WHY DON'T YOU TRADE YOURSELF?

WELL, WE LOST THE FIRST GAME OF THE SEASON AGAIN!

I SHOULDN'T LET IT BOTHER ME, BUT IT DOES...

WE ALWAYS SEEM TO LOSE THE FIRST GAME OF THE SEASON AND THE LAST GAME OF THE SEASON..

AND ALL THE STUPID GAMES IN-BETWEEN!

IS THIS YOUR BAT, CHARLIE BROWN? IT DOESN'T HAVE YOUR NAME ON IT...

YOU SHOULD HAVE YOUR NAME ON YOURS LIKE ALL OF THE BIG LEAGUE PLAYERS

LINUS HAS A WOOD-BURNING SET AT HOME... WHY DON'T I TAKE YOUR BAT, AND PUT YOUR NAME ON IT?

SAY! THIS IS GOING TO BE GREAT!

I'LL BE THE ONLY ONE AROUND HERE WITH HIS NAME ON A BAT!

THIS WILL REALLY IMPRESS THE KIDS ON THE OTHER TEAMS WE PLAY...THEY'LL BE AFRAID TO SEE ME STEP UP TO THE PLATE... THEY'LL THINK I'M A BIG-LEAGUER, AND I'LL...

HERE'S YOUR BAT, CHARLIE BROWN!

I HAD A LITTLE TROUBLE WITH THE WOOD-BURNING SET...

SCHULZ

THERE'S MORE TO LIFE THAN PLAYING BASEBALL!

THAT'S THE SORT OF THING THAT CAN THROW YOUR TIMING OFF

HEY, MANAGER, DO YOU THINK THIS GAME WILL BE OVER BY DARK?

I HOPE SO.....WHY?

I HAVE NO DESIRE TO BE CHOMPED BY A NIGHT SNAKE!

A NIGHT SNAKE?

ONCE YOU GET CHOMPED BY A NIGHT SNAKE, YOU'VE HAD IT!

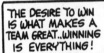    

STRIKE THREE!

THIS BAT IS NO GOOD! IT'S TOO LIGHT! THAT BALL THEY'RE USING IS NO GOOD EITHER!

HOW CAN ANYBODY HIT WHEN THE SUN IS SO BRIGHT? I BAT BETTER WHEN IT'S CLOUDY! IT'S TOO DUSTY OUT THERE, TOO!

I CAN'T HIT WELL WHEN THE WIND IS BLOWING! THAT BAT I WAS USING IS TOO SHORT! IT'S HARD TO SEE THE BALL TODAY! YOU CAN'T HIT A BALL WHEN THE BAT IS TOO THIN! I THINK THEIR PITCHER IS..

GOOD GRIEF!

WELL, WE LOST AGAIN

LUCY, DO ME A FAVOR...

ASK OUR PLAYERS TO LINE UP TO SHAKE HANDS WITH THE OTHER TEAM AND SAY, "NICE GAME"

OKAY, TEAM, IT'S HYPOCRITE TIME!!

HERE, CHARLIE BROWN... SIGN THIS PETITION!

WHAT'S IT FOR?

DON'T BE SO WISHY-WASHY.. JUST SIGN IT!

WANTING TO KNOW WHAT YOU'RE SIGNING IS NOT BEING WISHY-WASHY!

WHY ARE YOU SO CRABBY?

YELLING AT SOMEONE WHO SAYS YOU'RE WISHY-WASHY FOR WANTING TO KNOW WHAT YOU'RE SIGNING BEFORE YOU SIGN IT, IS NOT BEING CRABBY!!

ALL RIGHT, IF I LET YOU READ IT, WILL YOU SIGN IT?

"WE, THE UNDERSIGNED, THINK OUR MANAGER IS TOO WISHY-WASHY AND TOO CRABBY"

YOU PROMISED TO SIGN IT..

I'M THE ONLY PERSON I KNOW WHO'S EVER SIGNED A PETITION AGAINST HIMSELF

SCHULZ

THE FIRST BATTER HIT ONE OVER MY HEAD...

THE SECOND BATTER HIT ONE IN FRONT OF ME...

THE THIRD BATTER HIT ONE TO MY LEFT AND THE FOURTH BATTER HIT ONE TO MY RIGHT...

I'M LOOKING FORWARD TO THIS NEXT BATTER!

I'VE BEEN GOING OVER OUR BASEBALL STATISTICS FOR THIS PAST YEAR..

WHEN I THINK OF ALL THOSE GAMES WE LOST, I GET SICK..

WINNING ISN'T EVERYTHING, CHARLIE BROWN...

THAT'S TRUE, BUT LOSING ISN'T **ANYTHING**!

GOOD GRIEF! IT'S MORNING ALREADY!

THIS IS THE DAY OF OUR FIRST GAME

I'M NO MANAGER...I CAN'T RUN A BASEBALL TEAM...EVERYBODY KNOWS I'M A LOUSY MANAGER... NOBODY EVEN PAYS ANY ATTENTION TO ME...THEY ALL HATE ME...

I THINK I'LL JUST STAY IN BED... MAYBE IT'LL RAIN...MAYBE NO ONE ELSE WILL SHOW UP EITHER... I'LL JUST STAY IN BED, AND...

OKAY, MANAGER! RISE, AND SHINE!

I CAN'T GO OUT THERE TODAY, LUCY.. I'M NO GOOD AS A MANAGER..I'M SCARED!

SCARED? WHY, YOU BLOCKHEAD!

YOU WANTED TO BE THE MANAGER, AND YOU'RE GOING TO BE THE MANAGER! NOW, YOU GET OUT THERE AND MANAGE!!!

BOOT

HI, CHARLIE BROWN! WHERE HAVE YOU BEEN? WE'VE BEEN WAITING FOR YOU...

WELL, AT FIRST I THOUGHT I WOULDN'T BE ABLE TO MAKE IT, BUT I FINALLY GOT HERE UNDER THE INFLUENCE OF INFLUENCE!

LUCY! WAKE UP!

Z

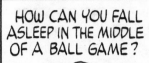

HOW CAN YOU FALL ASLEEP IN THE MIDDLE OF A BALL GAME?

SORRY, MANAGER... WATCHING YOUR GRACEFUL MOVES ON THE PITCHER'S MOUND LULLED ME TO SLEEP!

YES, I CAN SEE HOW THAT MIGHT HAPPEN...

SCHULZ

YOU THINK YOU'D BE HAPPY IF YOU WON A BALL GAME, DON'T YOU, CHARLIE BROWN?

THE DOCTOR IS IN

WELL, YOU WOULDN'T! IF YOU WON ONE GAME, YOU'D WANT TO WIN ANOTHER, AND THEN ANOTHER!

SOON YOU'D WANT TO WIN EVERY BALL GAME YOU PLAYED...

YEAHHH!!

SCHULZ

JOE DI MAGGIO NEVER COMPLAINED ABOUT PLAYING BALL ON A HOT DAY!

WHO WAS JOE DI MAGGIO?

ONE OF THE GREATEST OUTFIELDERS WHO EVER LIVED, THAT'S WHO!

I THOUGHT HE JUST DRANK COFFEE

WELL, OL' FAITHFUL GLOVE, ANOTHER SEASON HAS COME AND GONE... I GUESS I'LL PUT YOU AWAY UNTIL NEXT SPRING...

✻SIGH✻ THERE I WAS, A BEAUTIFUL PIECE OF GENUINE LEATHER...

SO WHAT HAPPENS? I END UP AS A BASEBALL GLOVE FOR A STUPID KID WHO LOSES EVERY GAME HE PITCHES!

OF COURSE, IT MIGHT HAVE BEEN WORSE... I COULD HAVE BEEN A PAIR OF GOALIE PADS AND GOT HIT BY PUCKS ALL WINTER...

STRIKE THREE

GOOD GRIEF, SHE STRUCK OUT AGAIN! THAT'S THREE TIMES SO FAR... I SHOULD SAY SOMETHING TO HER...AFTER ALL, I'M THE MANAGER...

BUT IF I SAY ONE WORD, SHE'LL BLOW SKY HIGH...SHE'S SO MAD NOW SHE'S READY TO BUST...I DON'T DARE MAKE A SOUND...

OH, OH! MY THROAT'S GETTING DRY...I'VE GOT TO CLEAR MY THROAT...

BUT IF I MAKE JUST THE SLIGHTEST SOUND, SHE'LL THINK I'M GOING TO SAY SOMETHING TO HER...

BUT I'VE GOT TO CLEAR MY THROAT...I...I... GULP! I'VE GOT TO COUGH OR GO "AHEM" OR SOMETHING...MY THROAT FEELS SO DRY...I...I...

AHEM!

I DIDN'T STRIKE OUT ON PURPOSE!

WE MANAGERS HAVE A ROUGH LIFE...

SCHULZ

ONE FINGER WILL MEAN A STRAIGHT BALL, TWO FINGERS WILL MEAN A STRAIGHT BALL, THREE FINGERS WILL MEAN A STRAIGHT BALL AND FOUR FINGERS WILL MEAN A STRAIGHT BALL...

I HAVE A VERY SARCASTIC CATCHER

HEY, MANAGER, MY GLOVE IS SO STIFF I CAN'T CATCH THE BALL!

THAT'S BECAUSE YOU HAVEN'T USED IT ALL WINTER...TRY RUBBING A LITTLE NEAT'S-FOOT OIL INTO IT

FORGET IT!

I HATE ANY SPORT WHERE YOU HAVE TO TAKE CARE OF YOUR EQUIPMENT!

I'VE BEEN THINKING ABOUT SOMETHING...

IN THE BIG LEAGUES, WHEN A TEAM GETS A RALLY STARTED, SOMEONE BLOWS A TRUMPET AND EVERYONE YELLS, "CHARGE!!"

DO YOU THINK WE COULD DO THAT, CHARLIE BROWN?

I DON'T KNOW...WE'VE NEVER HAD A RALLY...

DID YOU SEE HOW I STRUCK OUT THAT LAST KID? PRETTY GOOD PITCHING, HUH?

YEAH, THAT WAS THAT KID WHO'S BEEN SICK IN BED ALL WINTER..HIS DOCTOR SAYS HE'S GOING TO BE ALL RIGHT, BUT TO GET OUT IN THE SUN...

HE ALSO DOESN'T SEE VERY WELL, AND HE'S NEVER PLAYED BASEBALL BEFORE...

SOMETIMES A CATCHER CAN KNOW TOO MUCH ABOUT THE OPPOSITION...

ALL RIGHT, SNOOPY, THIS IS THE LAST OF THE NINTH...WE NEED ONE RUN TO TIE UP THE GAME..

I WANT YOU TO GO UP THERE WITH TEETH-GRITTING DETERMINATION, AND GET ON BASE! LET'S SEE YOU GRIT YOUR TEETH...

THAT'S FINE...KEEP GRITTING YOUR TEETH, AND YOU'LL GET A HIT!

I FEEL LIKE A FOOL...

LOOK AT THAT! LINUS GOT A HIT, TOO! I KNEW WE STILL HAD A CHANCE!

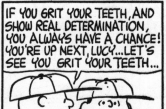

IF YOU GRIT YOUR TEETH, AND SHOW REAL DETERMINATION, YOU ALWAYS HAVE A CHANCE! YOU'RE UP NEXT, LUCY...LET'S SEE YOU GRIT YOUR TEETH...

FANTASTIC! YOU'LL SCARE THEIR PITCHER TO DEATH! KEEP GRITTING YOUR TEETH, AND GO GET A HIT!

GET A HIT?! I CAN'T EVEN SEE WHERE I'M GOING..

STRIKE ONE!

OOOOOO! C'MON, CHARLIE BROWN, **HIT IT**! FOR ONCE IN YOUR LIFE, **HIT IT**!!

WOULDN'T YOU LIKE JUST FOR ONCE TO SEE CHARLIE BROWN HIT THAT BALL?

NO..

I'M NOT PREPARED TO HAVE THE WORLD COME TO AN END!

STRIKE TWO!

NOW, I'M GOING TO GRIT MY TEETH, AND BEAR DOWN! IF A PERSON GRITS HIS TEETH, AND SHOWS REAL DETERMINATION, HE CAN'T FAIL!

STRIKE THREE!

YOU BLOCKHEAD!

YOUR TROUBLE, CHARLIE BROWN, IS THAT YOU LIVE BY MOTTOS AND TRITE SAYINGS..

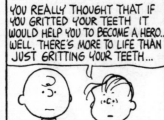
YOU REALLY THOUGHT THAT IF YOU GRITTED YOUR TEETH IT WOULD HELP YOU TO BECOME A HERO.. WELL, THERE'S MORE TO LIFE THAN JUST GRITTING YOUR TEETH...

CHARLIE BROWN, DO YOU UNDERSTAND WHAT I'M TRYING TO TELL YOU?

MAYBE I DIDN'T GRIT THEM HARD ENOUGH....MAYBE IF I...

SIGH!

WHAT ARE YOU DOING, CHARLIE BROWN?

I'M TRYING TO FIGURE OUT MY PITCHING RECORD FOR THIS YEAR..

YOU TAKE THE NUMBER OF EARNED RUNS, AND MULTIPLY BY NINE AND THEN DIVIDE BY THE NUMBER OF INNINGS PITCHED

WHAT DID YOU GET?

A FIGURE MUCH TOO EMBARRASSING TO MENTION!

SCHULZ

BONK!

AAUGH!

LUCY! HOW COULD YOU MISS THAT BALL?! IT CAME RIGHT TO YOU! HOW COULD YOU MISS IT?!!

I NEVER THINK ABOUT THE PAST

HEY, MANAGER, ARE WE SUPPOSED TO YELL, "I GOT IT!" OR "I HAVE IT!"?

IT DOESN'T MATTER, LUCY

I THINK HE'S RIGHT

KLUNK!

IF YOU DON'T GOT IT, YOU DON'T HAVE IT!

WELL, THAT DOES IT FOR ANOTHER SEASON, MANAGER! NOW, YOU HAVE TWO CHOICES..

YOU CAN GO HOME AND BROOD ABOUT THIS SEASON ALL WINTER LONG, OR YOU CAN LIE HERE AND ROT!

THOSE ARE GREAT CHOICES

I'M GLAD THE BASEBALL SEASON IS OVER FOR US!

I DON'T EVEN WANT TO HEAR THE WORD 'BASEBALL' ANY MORE! I THINK IF I HEAR THE WORD 'BASEBALL' AGAIN, I'LL SCREAM!

BASEBALL

AAUGH!

SEE THIS FIVE DOLLARS? I'M GOING TO SPEND IT ALL ON BUBBLE GUM CARDS! I'VE **GOT** TO GET A PICTURE OF **JOE SHLABOTNIK**!

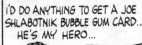

FIVE DOLLARS' WORTH OF BUBBLE GUM, PLEASE!

I'D DO ANYTHING TO GET A JOE SHLABOTNIK BUBBLE GUM CARD.. HE'S MY HERO...

FIVE DOLLARS' WORTH OF BUBBLE GUM, AND NOT ONE JOE SHLABOTNIK!

A PENNY'S WORTH OF BUBBLE GUM, PLEASE..

WELL, WHAT DO YOU KNOW...JOE SHLABOTNIK!

I THINK THEY'RE BEGINNING TO GET TO ME...I NEED A NEW PITCH OR SOMETHING...WHAT DO YOU THINK I NEED, SCHROEDER?

A CONCRETE PILLBOX!

I'M GONNA STEAL HOME, AND I'M GONNA BE A HERO!

GET READY NOW....HERE I GO...DON'T BE A COWARD....HERE I GO...DON'T BE SCARED...

HERE I GO....ZOOM....HERE I GO...DON'T BE A COWARD...HERE I GO...DON'T BE SCARED...

HERE I STAY!

I GOTTA TRY IT!

IF I'M GONNA BE A **HERO**, I GOTTA TRY TO STEAL HOME!

FIRST I'LL DANCE AROUND A LITTLE ON THE BASELINE TO CONFUSE THEIR PITCHER...

...AND THEN I'LL...

TAKE OFF!

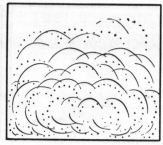

IF THIS WERE SUMMER, I'D BE STANDING OUT HERE ON THIS MOUND GETTING READY TO PITCH..

I'D LOOK IN AT MY CATCHER... I'D GET THE SIGN...

THE WINDUP!

THE PITCH!

POW! IT'S A DRIVE TO DEEP CENTER

AND YOU CAN TELL THAT ONE GOOD-BYE!

EVEN MY WINTERS ARE SUMMERS!

AAUGH! A SPIDER!!

THERE'S A SPIDER ON THE BALL! WE CAN'T PICK UP THE BALL, CHARLIE BROWN! THERE'S A SPIDER ON IT!

IT WILL BE INTERESTING TO SEE IF THE OFFICIAL SCORER GIVES THE HITTER CREDIT FOR A HOME RUN..

KLOP!

I WONDER WHY HE WEARS A GLOVE...

WHERE ELSE WOULD I KEEP MY LUNCH?

HAVE YOU EVER NOTICED HOW THE PEOPLE IN THE STANDS REALLY DON'T KNOW WHAT WE'RE SAYING WHEN WE HAVE THESE CONFERENCES ON THE MOUND?

ALL THEY HAVE TO GO BY IS THE WAY WE WAVE OUR ARMS

SEE, I POINT TO THE OUTFIELD, AND THEY THINK I'M TALKING ABOUT SOMETHING OUT THERE...

OR I CAN HOLD UP TWO FINGERS, AND THEY THINK I'M SAYING THAT THERE'S TWO OUTS NOW, AND WE HAVE TO GET THIS NEXT HITTER...

NO ONE IN THE STANDS CAN TELL WHAT I'M REALLY SAYING...

WHAT IS IT THAT YOU'RE REALLY SAYING?

I THINK YOU'RE KIND OF CUTE!

I CAN'T STAND IT!

☆ SIGH ☆

♪

HEY, MANAGER, WHAT DO THEY MEAN WHEN THEY SAY, "JUST WAIT 'TIL NEXT YEAR"?

THEY MEAN THAT ALTHOUGH THEIR TEAM WASN'T VERY GOOD THIS YEAR, NEXT YEAR THEY'RE GOING TO BE BETTER

JUST WAIT 'TIL TWENTY YEARS FROM NOW!

LUCY, WE'VE GOT TO GET A RUNNER ON BASE...

I DON'T SUPPOSE YOU'D LET YOURSELF GET HIT ON THE HEAD WITH THE BALL, WOULD YOU?

THIS IS THE FIRST TIME I'VE EVER LOOKED DIRECTLY INTO THE EYES OF SOMEONE WHO IS TOTALLY OUT OF HIS MIND!

HEY, MANAGER..

NOW WHAT?

I THINK YOUR DOG IS AFRAID OF THUNDER

BONK

WHAT HAPPENED?

CHARLIE BROWN GOT HIT WITH A LINE-DRIVE!

DOES ANYONE HERE KNOW ANYTHING ABOUT FIRST-AID?

IT'S PROBABLY NOT SERIOUS.. SECOND OR THIRD-AID WILL DO

I HATE IT WHEN THE BASEBALL SEASON IS OVER

THERE'S A DREARINESS IN THE AIR THAT DEPRESSES ME...

EVERYTHING SEEMS SAD...EVEN THE OL' PITCHER'S MOUND IS COVERED WITH WEEDS...

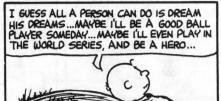

I GUESS ALL A PERSON CAN DO IS DREAM HIS DREAMS...MAYBE I'LL BE A GOOD BALL PLAYER SOMEDAY...MAYBE I'LL EVEN PLAY IN THE WORLD SERIES, AND BE A HERO...

? I BET I WILL PLAY IN THE WORLD SERIES SOMEDAY...I BET I'LL...

HEY! LOOK WHO'S OUT HERE TALKING TO HIMSELF!

WHAT ARE YOU DOING, CHARLIE BROWN, THINKING ABOUT ALL THE TIMES YOU STRUCK OUT?!

THERE'S A DREARINESS IN THE AIR THAT DEPRESSES ME!

SCHULZ

Panel 1: HOW SHALL WE PITCH THIS NEXT GUY, CHARLIE BROWN? / WELL, I DON'T KNOW.. / THROW HIM YOUR CURVE, CHARLIE BROWN

Panel 2: SAY, HAVE YOU NOTICED HOW BUILT-UP IT'S GETTING AROUND HERE? PRETTY SOON THERE WON'T BE ANY PLACE FOR US TO PLAY..LOOK AT ALL THE HOUSES...

Panel 3: MY GRAMPA SAYS THAT ALL OF THIS USED TO BE A BIG PASTURE..

Panel 4: HE SAYS HE CAN REMEMBER WHEN THEY USED TO DRIVE CATTLE RIGHT ACROSS HERE / MY DAD SAYS HE COULD HAVE MADE A LOT OF MONEY IF HE HAD BOUGHT THIS LAND TWENTY YEARS AGO

Panel 5: TWENTY YEARS AGO? FIVE YEARS AGO WOULD HAVE BEEN ENOUGH! / THAT'S WHAT I SAY! / OF COURSE! LAND VALUES ARE GOING UP EVERYWHERE

Panel 6: LOOK AT THAT PLACE WHERE THEY PUT UP THE NEW SUPER-MARKET.. / THAT'S WHAT MY GRAMPA WAS TALKING ABOUT..HE SAID YOU COULD HAVE BOUGHT THAT PROPERTY FOR ALMOST NOTHING ONLY TWO YEARS AGO!

Panel 7: WHAT DO YOU THINK, CHARLIE BROWN?

Panel 8: FRANKLY, I THINK HE'D HIT A CURVE BALL...

SCHULZ

OKAY, START THE GAME!

I FEEL BETTER! I'VE STOPPED SHAKING!

THE GAME'S OVER, CHARLIE BROWN, AND GUESS WHAT... **WE WON!**

LINUS TOOK YOUR PLACE... HE PITCHED A GREAT GAME... AND THERE WAS THIS LITTLE RED-HAIRED GIRL WATCHING...

SHE GOT SO EXCITED AFTER THE GAME THAT SHE RUSHED OUT TO THE MOUND, AND GAVE LINUS A BIG HUG!

AAUGH!

MY FRIEND

MY FRIEND, THE RELIEF PITCHER

MY FRIEND, THE RELIEF PITCHER, WHO PITCHED A GREAT GAME, AND IMPRESSED THAT LITTLE RED-HAIRED GIRL SO MUCH THAT SHE RAN OUT AND GAVE HIM A BIG HUG!

MY FRIEND!

YOU HAVE A JOE SHLABOTNIK? YOU HAVE A JOE SHLABOTNIK BUBBLE GUM CARD?

HE'S MY FAVORITE PLAYER! I'VE BEEN TRYING TO GET HIM ON A BUBBLE GUM CARD FOR FIVE YEARS! YOU WANNA TRADE?

HERE...I'LL GIVE YOU WHITEY FORD, MICKEY MANTLE, ROBIN ROBERTS, LUIS APARICIO, BILL MONBOUQUETTE, DICK STUART AND JUAN PIZARRO!

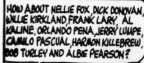

NO, I DON'T THINK SO...

HOW ABOUT NELLIE FOX, DICK DONOVAN, WILLIE KIRKLAND, FRANK LARY, AL KALINE, ORLANDO PENA, JERRY LUMPE, CAMILO PASCUAL, HARMON KILLEBREW, BOB TURLEY AND ALBIE PEARSON?

NO I DON'T WANT TO TRADE..I THINK JOE SHLABOTNIK IS KIND OF CUTE..

I'LL GIVE YOU TOM CHENEY, CHUCK COTTIER, WILLIE MAYS, ORLANDO CEPEDA, MAURY WILLS, SANDY KOUFAX, FRANK ROBINSON, BOB PURKEY, BILL MAZEROSKI, HARVEY HADDIX, WARREN SPAHN, HANK AARON, TONY GONZALES, ART MAHAFFEY, ROGER CRAIG, DUKE SNIDER, DON NOTTEBART, AL SPANGLER, CURT SIMMONS, STAN MUSIAL, ERNIE BANKS AND LARRY JACKSON!

NO, I DON'T THINK SO..

FOR FIVE YEARS I'VE BEEN TRYING TO GET A JOE SHLABOTNIK! MY FAVORITE BASEBALL PLAYER, AND I CAN'T GET HIM ON A BUBBLE GUM CARD... FIVE YEARS! MY FAVORITE PLAYER...

HE'S NOT AS CUTE AS I THOUGHT HE WAS!

THERE'S MORE TO PLAYING RIGHT FIELD THAN CHEWING GUM AND BLOWING BUBBLES!

BONK!

LIKE WHAT?

COME BACK, EVERYBODY! WE CAN STILL PLAY!

A LITTLE WATER DOESN'T HURT!

THE WAVES AREN'T THAT HIGH!

THERE AREN'T EVEN ANY WHITE CAPS!

THERE'S A FULL MOON TONIGHT, BIG BROTHER..

YOU SHOULD GO OUT, AND LOOK AT IT

MAYBE I WILL...THANK YOU..

I MISS THE BASEBALL SEASON...

I MISS STANDING OUT HERE ON THE PITCHER'S MOUND WITH THE EXCITEMENT OF THE GAME ALL AROUND ME...

LADIES AND GENTLEMEN, THE LINEUPS FOR TODAY'S GAME...

INDULGING IN A LITTLE FANTASY, EH, CHARLIE BROWN? OKAY, LET'S PRETEND I'M THE CATCHER...

ALL RIGHT, PITCHER...WE'VE GOT TO GET OUR SIGNALS STRAIGHT....ONE FINGER WILL MEAN A FAST BALL, TWO FINGERS WILL MEAN A CURVE AND YOU KNOW WHAT THREE FINGERS WILL MEAN?

THREE FINGERS WILL MEAN A SNOWBALL! HA! HA! HA! HA! HA!

HER KIND KNOWS NO SEASON!

WHICH IS CORRECT, "WHO ARE WE KIDDING?" OR "WHOM ARE WE KIDDING?"

WELL, I SUPPOSE "WHOM" IS CORRECT ALTHOUGH MOST PEOPLE WOULD SAY "WHO"

WHAT DO YOU THINK OUR CHANCES ARE OF WINNING TODAY?

OH, I'D SAY ABOUT FIFTY-FIFTY...

WHOM ARE WE KIDDING?

POW!

LOOK, CHARLIE BROWN... I CAUGHT YOUR SHOE!

MAYBE I SHOULD PITCH MY SHOE INSTEAD OF THE BALL...

THAT'S A GOOD IDEA.. GIVE 'EM THE OL' KNUCKLE SHOE!

THE WEATHER SURE HAS BEEN BAD LATELY

DON'T CRITICIZE THE WORLD, CHARLIE BROWN!

"WHERE WERE YOU WHEN HE LAID THE FOUNDATION OF THE EARTH? WHO LAID ITS CORNERSTONE WHEN ITS MORNING STARS SANG TOGETHER?"

"WHO SHUT IN THE SEA WITH DOORS WHEN IT BURST FORTH FROM THE WOMB? HAVE YOU ENTERED THE STOREHOUSE OF THE SNOW?"

"WHO CAN NUMBER THE CLOUDS BY WISDOM? OR WHO CAN TILT THE WATERSKINS OF THE HEAVENS?"

"IS THE WILD OX WILLING TO SERVE YOU? DO YOU GIVE THE HORSE HIS MIGHT? IS IT BY YOUR WISDOM THAT THE HAWK SOARS, AND SPREADS HIS WINGS TOWARD THE SOUTH?"

DON'T CRITICIZE THE WORLD, CHARLIE BROWN

HOW WOULD IT BE IF I JUST YELLED AT THE UMPIRE?

HEY, MANAGER!

I'VE DECIDED THAT I SHOULD BE PAID A MILLION DOLLARS A YEAR

BRRATRRR!!

SO MUCH FOR ARBITRATION...

YOU KNOW WHAT?

THE LAST PIANO OWNED BY BEETHOVEN HAS BEEN SENT TO NUERNBERG FOR RESTORATION

THAT'S VERY INTERESTING

MY CATCHER HAS MANY THINGS ON HIS MIND!

BEFORE WE START THE GAME, CHARLIE BROWN, YOU HAVE TO ASK THE BALL IF IT WANTS TO PLAY..

I HAVE TO **WHAT?**

YOU HAVE TO ASK THE BALL IF IT WANTS TO PLAY! YOU ASKED THE OTHER TEAM, DIDN'T YOU? AND YOU ASKED ALL OF YOUR OWN PLAYERS, DIDN'T YOU? OF COURSE, YOU DID!

NOW, YOU HAVE TO ASK THE BALL! AFTER ALL, THE BALL IS THE ONE WHO'S GOING TO GET HIT ALL THE TIME, ISN'T IT? DON'T YOU THINK IT SHOULD HAVE A CHOICE?

GO AHEAD, CHARLIE BROWN...ASK THE BALL.. ASK THE BALL IF IT WANTS TO PLAY...

I FEEL LIKE A FOOL

HEY, BALL..DO YOU WANT TO PLAY IN THE GAME TODAY?

IT DIDN'T ANSWER

IT'S TRYING TO MAKE UP ITS MIND...I GUESS I'LL GO HOME...

GO HOME?!

I'M NOT GOING TO STAND AROUND ALL DAY WHILE SOME STUPID BALL TRIES TO MAKE UP ITS MIND!

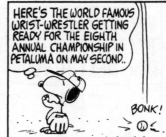